Twenty Leader Discovery Lessons

Twenty Most Memorable Blog Posts From 2015

Leader Discovery
www.leaderdiscovery.com
Suite 154 #201
7320 N La Cholla Blvd
Tucson, AZ 85741

520-505-5670

Twenty Leader Discovery Lessons

Twenty Most Memorable Blog Posts

Leader Discovery
www.leaderdiscovery.com
Suite 154 #201
7320 N La Cholla Blvd
Tucson, AZ 85741

Copyright © 2015 by Sandra Langford Abbey

All rights reserved. No part of this publication may be reproduced, distributed, or transmitted in any form or by any means, including photocopying, recording, or other electronic or mechanical methods, without the prior written permission of the author, except in the case of brief quotations embodied in critical reviews and certain other noncommercial uses permitted by copyright law.

CONTENTS

1. Finding Your Leadership Pathway   07
2. Reasons Leaders Should Not Set New Year's Resolutions   09
3. Is It Time For A Strategic Plan Update?   13
4. Why Should Solo HR Professionals Join Mastermind Groups?   17
5. Leaders Need To Get Over The "It's The Economy" Excuse   21
6. Top Challenges Facing HR And Business Executives   25
7. Leadership Lessons From A Shallow River   27
8. Leadership And Competitive Sports   31
9. Steps To Embed Leadership Into Succession Planning   33
10. Emerging Leaders   37

CONTENTS CONTINUED

11. Why Are Half Your Employees Floundering?   39
12. Reasons Employees Quit   43
13. Leadership Is Never Manipulative   45
14. The Courage To Be Vulnerable   47
15. Ways Leaders Create Trust   51
16. Leaders Should Harvest What They Sow   57
17. Thanksgiving And Leadership   61
18. Things Top Companies Do To Develop Leaders   63
19. Steps To Creating A Leadership Development Program   67
20. Elements To Include In Your Leadership Development Program   71

Twenty Leader Discovery Lessons
For
Subscribers to the Leader Discovery Blog

Dedication:

It was about one year ago that I made the decision to leave my very fulfilling, amazing, dream job and create a new company dedicated to filling the world with leaders. Once that decision was made, I worked tirelessly to establish Langford Abbey Ventures, Inc. under the trade name Leader Discovery.

Leader Discovery provides leadership and communication training and development programs for small to mid-sized organizations to help them transform their supervisors and managers into leaders so they can prosper, grow, and sustain their organizations in these times of incredible and rapid change.

Leader Discovery also provides organizational effectiveness, human resources, succession and workforce planning consulting services for small to mid-sized organizations that may not have full-time human resources functions or have staff members stretched thin and not able to tackle new programs and initiatives effectively while maintaining their day-to-day workload. We also work with organizations that sometimes desire a neutral third party to help them reflect, forecast, plan, and implement changes through our advanced facilitation services.

Leader Discovery supports individuals who strive to become their best selves through leadership and life coaching, small group mastermind programs, and events that allow personal reflection, goal setting, and motivation through making forward progress to achieve their objectives.

This book is a look back at our 20 most popular blog posts and is dedicated to you, our blog subscribers, whether you were with us from the beginning or have only recently subscribed. If you have not yet subscribed, visit our blog at www.leaderdiscovery.com to join our growing group of loyal readers and followers. Our future plans include bringing more content, more services, and more value to all our subscribers in the coming year! Thank you for your support and stay tuned for an amazing year to come.

Copyright © 2015 by Sandra Langford Abbey

All rights reserved. No part of this publication may be reproduced, distributed, or transmitted in any form or by any means, including photocopying, recording, or other electronic or mechanical methods, without the prior written permission of the author, except in the case of brief quotations embodied in critical reviews and certain other noncommercial uses permitted by copyright law.

1
Finding Your Own Leadership Pathway

Over many years of studying and observing leaders in a varicty of situations and working with some great leaders and some leaders aspiring to be great, it has become more clear to me that there is no one single pathway to leadership. There is not a magic formula for how to be a leader that once mastered and followed precisely will develop a person into greatness.

Instead, the key is to discover your own personal, individual leadership strengths. Don't try to copy someone else's style. Instead truly become self-aware, and develop those unique abilities that are your personal leadership gifts. Once you know who you are as a leader, it takes a tremendous amount of work and even courage to trust yourself to lead based on who you are rather than who others expect you to be.

Once this is mastered, the journey to leadership greatness begins. That's right. Self-awareness is only the beginning of the leadership journey.

Focus on growing and developing your strongest leadership attributes. Choose to serve those who follow you by using your leadership strengths. I firmly believe it is a continuous pathway – always a journey. You will never "arrive" because leaders never stop striving to grow, develop, learn, and serve those who follow.

Four common pathways to leadership are listed here. There is infinite variation on these because each journey is unique to the individual.

- Leadership through building relationships with others
- Leadership through creating systems and processes to guide others
- Leadership through helping others achieve results
- Leadership through motivating and inspiring others

2
Three Reasons Leaders Should Not Set New Year's Resolutions

Setting specific, measurable goals, then developing a plan to achieve those goals trumps New Year's resolutions every time.

1. Leaders who are self-aware know that continuous improvement is required year round. When changes must be made, waiting for an arbitrary date on the calendar to adjust actions, (personally or for your business), makes no sense. Instead, leaders should always look inwardly at bad habits or ineffective behaviors that need to change now – whenever now is. This self-reflection helps the leader to then look outwardly at others to discover what new behaviors and actions should replace the bad habits for more effective relationships. After all, developing relationships truly is the most valuable skill of a leader.

2. Leaders know a goal is reached only if strategy is well executed. Simply stating a goal, such as "I want to be more active next year," will not make it happen. Without the essence of a personal strategic plan with clear objectives and measurable, attainable targets, there is little reason to expect the goal will be achieved. Instead leaders should use their strategic planning skills to implement personal resolutions in the same way business or organizational goals are achieved. Using the example goal of "to be more active next year," a strategy might be to walk more. An objective to reach an average of 5,000 steps per day within 90 days, 10,000 steps per day within 120 days, and 12,000 steps per day by the end of the calendar year is specific, measurable, and attainable. The implementation plan could include using a pedometer each day to measure steps, recording the steps before going to bed each night, and reviewing the average steps per day at the end of each week. Setting New Year's resolutions is rarely successful, but developing a strategic

plan that is clear and actionable leads to success.

3. The past tends to repeat itself, and leaders are human beings with their preferred behavioral patterns, good and bad. To succeed changes must be sustainable and rewarding; otherwise, there is no reason to give up those preferred behavior patterns for new habits. Leaders who want sustainable and long-lasting change should work on only one personal change at a time. Make small, manageable adjustments, replacing bad habits with small changes that can be improved upon little-by-little. Use the information from self-reflection to choose what to change, and put together a personal strategic plan, such as the example above, that is achievable. Execute that plan to make sustainable change, instead of setting a New Year's resolution that will fade shortly after it is resolved.

*Photograph Courtesy of
Death To Stock Photographs*

3
Is It Time For A Strategic Plan Update?

You have a mission, vision, and values statement. They are on wall posters and placards, in your employee handbook, and displayed on your website. Do they drive your organization toward the future or help you manage the status quo?

If it's been more than two or three years since your last focused strategic planning retreat, your organization may be managing status quo. You might be doing that in a highly effective way. On the other hand, you may find a growing disconnect between day-to-day operations and trends you are beginning to see on the horizon. Continuing on the status quo path means those trends have a tendency to "sneak up on you," and even though you saw them, you suddenly realize the future trends are already here, and your organization is not prepared to take advantage of the opportunities or mitigate the threats brought by the changes.

Strategic planning retreats can be time consuming and can take away from the constant necessity for managing the operations of the organization. However, that is part of the reason it is so critical to take the time to step outside of operations, reflect on your past and current situation, and then plan for the future. Depending on your industry, and how frequently your management team has taken time out for planning, a focused retreat of even a half day can help. Others may need one or two full planning days.

The purpose of retreating offsite (or at least to an onsite conference room that gets your management team outside of the operational duties for the day) is the same reason to bring in a facilitator to guide the planning session. The facilitator provides an atmosphere of reflection and vision-casting that is the precursor to developing an operational implementation plan to move your organization toward its future.

As a strategic planning facilitator for Leader Discovery, one of the major rewards I see from serving clients in both for-profit and non-profit organizations during these retreat-style planning sessions is an amazing, shared clarity of purpose among management team members when they are freed up to really focus on the organization as a whole versus their individual functional area. The process brings management together into a true team and allows the facilitator to sometimes play devil's advocate to shed light on barriers that could be holding the organization back from capitalizing on future opportunities.

Photograph by Michael Sultzbach

4
Why Should Solo HR Professionals Join Mastermind Groups?

HR leaders in departments of one (or even those in departments of 2-3) are generally juggling work that is 20% strategic, organizational development work and 80% administrative and transactional work. With that type of imbalance it is difficult to take time to think, develop, grow, and focus on organizational effectiveness, or your own career for that matter.

Mastermind groups can cultivate business relationships based on trust with like-minded professionals who are struggling and succeeding in this role. Choosing business relationships with care and cultivating them into supportive groups that also hold you accountable will impact your personal and professional life in profound ways.

A small group of people, who we allow to see our most vulnerable and our most triumphant selves, can directly affect what we ultimately achieve in our careers. This is the power behind a mastermind group.

A small group of colleagues, friends, and confidantes pushes each group member to stretch beyond their comfort zone, work harder, think boldly, be there for each other for support when they feel like quitting, and hold each other accountable in a way that is inspirational.

What happens in a mastermind group?

The group is generally small – as few as six to eight members, and no more than 15 to 20 members is ideal. In larger groups the best thing to do is break the group into smaller circles of four to eight members who work closely together during the masterminding session. Most importantly, the group must form a solid and confidential connection, and must have a structured method or process for sharing anything from goals to accomplishments, challenges, results, projects, and struggles.

The group acts as an advisory board for each member by brainstorming ideas, sharing best practice suggestions, making recommendations, and providing advice. It is important that everyone in the group is able to give and receive feedback and advice openly and authentically.

If someone resists listening to or acting on the advice, then they are not ready for the growth and development that can be achieved by masterminding. Similarly, if someone always gives advice as the "expert," yet is never willing to listen to the advice of others, then that person is not a good fit for the mastermind group. Only a group in which everyone is equally able to give and receive advice, plus trust the other group members and gain the trust of the other members will allow the amazing power of masterminding to unfold.

Photograph by Randy Abbey

Abbey Family Photo Collection

5
Leaders Need To Get Over The "It's The Economy" Excuse

We all know the economy took a nosedive in 2008-2009 because of multiple global events, most notably involving home mortgage lenders and others who were far too heavily leveraged. That is not what this article is about. For the past five to seven years now we've heard countless speeches, blogs, articles, whitepapers, and all manner of communication start with the words "In these tough economic times..." Quite frankly, the economy has normalized, and many people simply have not accepted the fact.

Too many leaders keep waiting for economic growth that was seen in the past to "return" without realizing it will not return unless industry and government leaders take actions to foster a growth environment. Government regulation certainly seems to be increasing, and that is also a new normal. Business leaders need to accept that only their own actions to be intentional about growing the business is likely to change things. We all need to get over using the excuse that we'll grow "once the economy gets back to normal" and just start doing it now. I don't pretend to have all the answers but here are some things that businesses can do to help:

1. Start thinking about how to differentiate your product or service to both retain current customers and to expand your customer base. A strong brand can convey what makes your product better than the competition and can be marketed to not only your core customers, but also to new customers you never thought about in the past.

2. Update your marketing strategy. There are so many different marketing methods and modalities out there, and businesses need to be taking advantage of these fully. Don't make the assumption that your customers are not reading print media any longer, and don't make the assumption that they are not using social media and a variety of

electronic gadgets from laptops to tablets to smartphones. Tap into all methods and modes of reaching your current and future customers.

3. Provide standout service to every customer, client, business associate, community member, and potential customer. Hyper-competition means customers have more choices than ever for accessing your product or service. They will not have much patience or loyalty for a business that does not listen to them, provide high quality products and services, and correct problems quickly and courteously. To focus on customer service means hiring right, developing employees, and empowering your staff members to make decisions and do the right thing to solve customer problems.

4. Develop and engage your team. Employees who believe in your company, product, services, and customers, plus understand the business, and who have the authority

to do what is right for both the business and the customers are still your greatest asset. Hire employees who have a great track record for customer service, creative problem-solving, innovative thinking, and a desire to do right for the company. Then, allow employees to truly provide outstanding service without getting bogged down in red-tape (other than needing to comply with regulations that we all must ensure are taken care of). When you do this, your staff will amaze you with their creative, productive, and enthusiastic work ethic.

Abbey Family Photo Collection

6
Top Challenges Facing Human Resources and Business Executives

I was reminded recently of the Deloitte Global Human Capital Trends report released early in 2014. The challenges expressed by more than 2,500 human resources and business executives from hundreds of companies around the globe had nothing to do with the "old school" human resources functions such as benefits and pay administration, policy enforcement, compliance, and endless personnel paperwork. Those traditional personnel tasks are being automated, outsourced, or downplayed by savvy companies who know there are much more important challenges facing companies in the 21st century.

In the survey 70% to 86% of business executives believed HR leaders need to focus on the following areas:

- Leadership development was number one with 86% of businesses stating this is a top priority they expect from human resources.

- Retention and engagement of employees (79% want HR to focus on this)
- Re-skilling the HR department to focus on business strategic priorities versus transactional personnel functions (77%)
- Talent acquisition, and
- Workforce capability training (tied with 75%)
- Global talent management (72%)
- HR analytics (71%)
- Learning and development (70%)

These priorities provided part of the rationale for launching our business, naming it Leader Discovery, and focusing efforts on learning, development, training, motivating and engaging employees, providing human resources support, and especially leadership development. These are all areas we are reaching out to human resources professionals in order to provide partnerships that allow them to meet these top priority areas.

7
Leadership Lessons From A Shallow River

Sometimes being a leader means plunging into new territory or making decisions without all of the facts known. Still, being prepared with as much information as reasonably possible can help things go more smoothly.

On a recent half-day kayaking trip three friends and I were prepared for some, but not all of the snags we encountered. A bit more homework may have steered us to a different waterway; however, we would not have had the same physical workout.

We selected a 6-mile segment of the Gila River just north of Winkelman, Arizona. Three out of the four of us had floated this segment two years prior, and because there have recently been some good southern Arizona rainstorms we were hoping there would be sufficient water flow (remember, this is the Southern Arizona desert – not a ton of water sports to be had). We were well prepared with sunscreen, snacks, and plenty of drinking water, and we expected to be on the river about 3 hours – a nice leisurely paddle.

What we found is in spite of the recent rains, the reservoir upriver was not necessarily letting much water flow through the dam into the river, and we were a little too far downstream – hence – very shallow water, sometimes only a few inches. This meant several times we had to get out of the kayaks and physically carry them for several yards to slightly deeper water. This also means lots of rocks, mud, fallen tree branches and other snags in the water to be avoided.

While we enjoyed the company of friends, and got a well-rounded workout from not only paddling, but also walking and carrying the kayaks, the trip took us well over 4 hours and was much less leisurely than we'd expected. We know we could have done more planning and gathered more information about the stream and water flow conditions, which might have lead us to choose a different location. But we're glad we made the trip and feel it was a rewarding adventure.

All this reminded me of how leaders sometimes have to make decisions based on limited or partial information. Still, with good planning and gathering of the facts that are available plunging into new challenges can be very rewarding.

Abbey Family Photo Collection

Abbey Family Photo Collection

8
Leadership And Competitive Sports

Most human resources professionals or recruiters have struggled with interview questions that get to the heart of important characteristics such as work ethic, achievement mentality, teamwork, and leadership. To simply ask "do you have a hard-working, team oriented, leadership ethic?" will inevitably get the answer "Why, yes!" Yet the interviewer has no clearer understanding of these characteristics. Situational and behavior-based questions do a better job, but some interviewers are looking to drill more into the underlying personality to find out what drives and motivates a person. It's also important to ensure that any questions asked are valid and as unbiased as possible.

With these things in mind one of my new favorite interview questions is to ask about whether or not the individual ever participated in sports or other team or individual competition. A follow-up question could be related to whether the activity was recreational, community-based, or competitive (and the ideal answer to that question would depend on the nature of the position you are seeking to fill). From my own experience in raising two children who each gravitated toward different competitive sports programs, I discovered that when someone becomes passionate about a sport, hobby, or activity, they will work extremely hard to participate.

Knowing that a person loved soccer or baseball or jazz dance so much that they would practice up to 20 hours a week after school (and sometimes before school) just to achieve the next level in that activity tells a great deal about that individual's work ethic. Knowing from an interview that the person you eventually hire has been that involved and passionate about achieving something is important. The hard part for a leader then, is finding a way to ignite that motivation and passion for the work you expect from your newly hired team member.

9
Three Steps To Embed Leadership Development Into Succession Planning

Small to mid-sized companies often face the challenge of having shallow bench-strength. Most individuals in such companies wear multiple hats and don't have anyone backing them up. There is also a lack of institutional knowledge being handed down over the years of internal promotional opportunities. Gone are the days when employees stayed with the same employer for decades, working their way up through the ranks with clearly defined career paths and plenty of time to grow into future leadership roles.

There are several steps (here are three) that organizations can take to prepare their future leaders for the challenges they will face:

1. Determine what leadership and management competencies are key to successfully heading up the organization. These include the

Photograph Courtesy of Death To Stock Photographs

Abbey Family Photo Collection

competencies needed today and projected to be needed in the future.

2. Create and update job descriptions to include the key competencies identified. Then, design learning and development programs around the key leadership and management competencies selected. All types of skills training and leadership and organizational development programs will need to include one or more of these key competencies to embed them into the fabric and culture of the company.

3. Hire individuals who already exhibit the key competencies, or who clearly have the capability to develop the leadership competencies needed. Then begin developing newly hired staff along with existing staff to continue the culture changes required.

Companies with little bench-strength can take advantage of succession planning when it is focused not only on top executives, but also includes developing

leadership competenc
organization. Consid
contributors, supervi
executives to become
role or position with
help ensure high pot
succeed when called

The exact future po
may be unknown, ye
skills to adapt, think
decisions, and m
changes. This is wl
than ever for cor
leadership training ;
individuals and wor
the current formal
the organization.

10
Emerging Leaders

Many parts of the country are still covered in snow, yet late February to early March is the time when we start seeing signs of Spring (and spring fever). This is the time of year when in between the last lingering winter storms, there are a few beautiful, sunny days that hint at what's in store when Spring hits in full force. Emerging leadership is like this - sometimes hiding in the midst of day-to-day activities, yet at times breaking out to show the sunny possibilities before becoming obscure again.

So how is a manager or mentor to help an emerging leader in this early stage? First, recognize and point out those glimmers and glimpses of leadership when they occur; second, support and reward the budding leadership behaviors; and third, never criticize or diminish attempts at leadership even if they are under developed or inconsistent or sometimes falter.

Be watchful for emerging leadership traits from your employees or protégés. Catch them being innovative, trying something new, weighing alternatives before making a decision, collaborating with others, or taking responsible risks.

When these glimmers and glimpses of leadership happen, make sure to notice, give praise, provide support, and coach the emerging leader to keep up the good work. And never introduce negativity, criticize or tell the employee to stop thinking, trying, and acting. If an emerging leadership trait disappears (as with one of those last lingering winter storms in March) coach, guide, and develop the employee so they know it is okay to learn from the situation and do better next time.

Abbey Family Photo Collection

11
Why Are Half Your Employees Floundering And What Can You Do About It?

I was shocked to learn from the 2014 Kelly Global Workforce Index (a survey of more than 200,000 employees) that 57% said they would prefer more training over a pay increase. Also, only 29% of employees said they had a clear career path with their current organization, and only 35% thought they had any chance of advancing in their company.

These numbers show that in spite of some recent increases in training and leadership development budgets occurring in some companies, most organizations are still not focusing on growing, developing, and advancing their human talent. Even employees who are promoted from within often face challenges that come from a lack of training and development to help them succeed in their new role with the organization. After all they were likely promoted for their highly developed technical skills at the previous job, not for management and leadership abilities.

So, what can be done about this problem?

First, supervisors and managers need to talk with their employees about their work performance, goals, and career aspirations (both within the company and externally). This should be done at least a couple of times per year - probably in conjunction with any formal performance evaluation or goal setting systems the organization has in place. If the company does not have any performance management program, the supervisor can add this to his or her staff coaching and development program for the department or team.

If the supervisor does not have the skills and capabilities to facilitate these career coaching discussions with her employees, the supervisor may wish to take advantage of leadership or coaching training programs. Another solution is to partner with a consultant who does career, work, or life coaching. The coach can be brought in to assist employees with career and current performance decisions. This is especially helpful for employees who may not have advancement opportunities within the company, yet cannot see these limitations and needs an outside perspective to help them recognize the need to move on.

Second, when an organization promotes an employee for his or her technical skills, capabilities, and competencies for the job he or she is currently in, the company must recognize the need to provide training, development, and management coaching for the newly promoted employee. That employee may be great at his prior job, but that does not mean he knows how to be a supervisor or manager. Group training when many supervisors and managers are in this situation is a great option, and can often be tailored specifically for the needs of the organization. Or if there is only one supervisor, manager, or executive who needs individualized training a professional or leadership and life coach can be very beneficial.

*Photograph Courtesy of
Death To Stock Photographs*

12
Five Reasons Employees Quit

Last year the human resources software company, BambooHR, surveyed more than 1,000 full-time workers in the U.S. to determine the top reasons employees quit their jobs. We've all heard the clichéd saying that employees don't quit their jobs, they quit their supervisors. This is still the top reason in this survey, yet there are five reasons listed that employers will want to consider:

1. Supervisors who don't empower the employee, or who make the employee feel they are not trusted.
2. Being asked to work on vacation or after hours, especially checking emails or voicemails.
3. Supervisors who blame employees when things go wrong.
4. No flexibility in scheduling, especially when employees need to take care of family responsibilities.
5. Co-workers who make the workplace intolerable.

One of the surprises here for me was the lack of flexibility and lack of family friendly policies. Work flexibility and work-life balance have been buzz words for at least 20-years, yet the majority of companies appear to be resistant to embracing these concepts or giving them more than lip service. I also wonder if this is partly because of antiquated labor and wage laws that don't support flexible scheduling even when it is the best solution for employees. The influx of the generation known as millennials may finally be what is needed to shift organizations toward flexibility.

13
Leadership Is Never Manipulative

The simple textbook definition of leadership is the ability to achieve a goal by influencing others. Another defines a leader as someone whom others choose to follow. These definitions can be supported by either a leader-centric or a follower-centric viewpoint. The leader-centric viewpoint holds that the knowledge, skills, traits, or capabilities of a great leader are such that others will work to achieve the desired goal. The follower-centric viewpoint supports the idea that followers willingly and faithfully will carry out anything necessary to further a goal through their devotion or belief in the end result to be achieved. In either case leaders and followers find themselves at the finish-line through a mutual understanding of the goal, what it will take to achieve that goal, support for the end result, and hard work toward completion.

In the above scenario there is no manipulation involved. If a person has an agenda or goal to advance, is not transparent in establishing a vision and direction for accomplishing the goal, and instead hides the true end result desired; then, any manipulative actions or deceptions that lead others to take steps toward the hidden goal cannot be considered to have occurred through leadership.

If others unwillingly or unknowingly advance another person's cause, they cannot be thought of as "followers" of the cause or of the person who has a hidden agenda. A person who happens to take an action without thought, or a person who is forced into taking an action without willingly choosing to do so, is not a supporter or follower. Because a leader by definition is someone whom others choose to follow, if a person is manipulated into furthering a goal and has not willingly chosen to follow someone, then no leadership has occurred. Consider this the next time you ask coworkers or employees to help you achieve a goal.

14
The Courage To Be Vulnerable

I was coaching a client who shared an experience he had at work that demonstrated his courage as a leader. To protect his identity and that of his employer, I'll call him Robert (not his real name). Robert recently switched to leading a new project team for an aerospace industry company. He confided in me that one of the engineers on the project seemed very hostile, distant, and defensive around him. The engineer used body language that clearly signaled he was mistrustful of Robert. The thing that really baffled my client is that he had only worked with this engineer for about two months, and Robert could not think of any time when he might have offended the engineer in a way that would have caused the defensiveness.

A day or two before the Christmas holidays this aerospace company was set to shutdown for the annual nearly two week break that is common in that industry during this time of year. Robert was trying to contact several members of the project team; however, he ran into a problem when he found most of the team members had already left early for the day (before noon). Robert found the engineer who had always acted defensively and asked where everyone was. The engineer reacted as expected – defensively - and reminded Robert that they had received permission from higher up the chain of command to check out by noon and charge the rest of the day to "overhead" versus to their project, so everyone was just following orders.

As they spoke, Robert showed vulnerability along with his frustration and confided in the engineer that he had never charged any time to "overhead" and had no idea how to do that. Suddenly, the engineer's eyes lit up, he smiled, and apparently realized that my demanding client didn't know everything and could use his help.

The engineer was happy to assist Robert in logging into the timekeeping system and showing him how to find the correct overhead charge account numbers. Robert didn't realize it at the time but this show of vulnerability and needing the help of the engineer ended up melting some of that defensiveness. This became even more evident after the holiday shut-down break. Robert was working with the engineer and found him to be much more open to sharing his thoughts, ideas, opinions and solutions to the project they were working on. The defensiveness seemed to be gone, and the tipping point to improving the relationship was simply that my client asked for help instead of issuing demands and edicts. After sharing this story, Robert and I discussed the fact that most people want to contribute their best work and may feel stifled if the project lead seems to have all the answers and never needs them to think critically, innovatively, and to solve problems. Most engineers I know get great satisfaction from solving problems. Robert plans to ask more questions and wait for the answers in the future, even if it means being vulnerable and showing his team that he doesn't know everything. This is a mark of leadership. As Ralph Waldo Emerson is credited with saying, "There is no limit to what can be accomplished if it doesn't matter who gets the credit."

Abbey Family Photo Collection

15
Four Ways Leaders Create Trust

A leader helps trust grow by communicating openly, listening for understanding, being authentic in action, and holding herself and others accountable.

1. Communicate openly and with a spirit of generosity and service to those who follow you. Whether or not you are a supervisor or manager to those you lead, or simply an organizational influencer, it is essential to establish trusting, give-and-take discussions with others. Share insights and your perspective to help develop trust among those who follow you. This creates a more connected and responsive group because everyone is on the same page. Leaders do this in order to serve others or the organization. It is not about showing off your knowledge. Building trust includes being highly collaborative, willingly sharing knowledge with others, giving your time and energy, and attending

to the contributions of followers. This produces a fluid collaboration not only of knowledge, but also insight and perspective. Leaders who communicate openly, sharing their knowledge, time and energy are seen as approachable, engaging, and thoughtful. These leaders take a personal interest in their followers and actively encourage them to become their best selves. They seek opportunities to see the best attributes and contributions of others through a more free-flowing communication process.

2. Listen to others, not only to hear what they say, but also to understand the meaning behind their words. Listening plays a critical role in establishing trust because it shows the leader's commitment to others. Both the leader and the organization grow when they consider the perspectives and concerns of their followers. When people in leadership roles listen attentively, they project empathy and show they are willing to consider the whole picture to

understand how others are affected. This all comes back to open and honest communication. It makes followers feel safe when they must reveal personal information, voice complaints, or try something new or untested. It is important to practice and improve listening skills and learn how to listen more deeply for understanding. This shows your followers you are acting with their best interests in mind.

3. Be courageous enough to know your own strengths and weaknesses, own who you really are, and accept that you must constantly improve and grow. This is the heart of being authentic. It takes courage and trust to be authentic. Authentic leaders take risks, step out of their comfort zone, and stop placing blame on others. These leaders transparently share both successes and failures. Leaders need to share not only what goes right, but also what goes wrong, so they can learn from their mistakes. It is not easy to share your failures as a leader with your

followers, but this could help others learn from your mistakes. Authentic leaders practice becoming self-aware and continuously seek to improve. This includes seeking 360-degree feedback, questioning their beliefs about themselves, and understanding the need to learn, grow, and develop.

4. Hold yourself accountable to do what you say you will do, and to hold others accountable for what they have committed to doing. This may go without saying, but it is so very important in building trust for a leader to always follow-through with what they say they will do. A leader also must firmly, yet empathetically, hold others accountable. Especially in a business setting many leaders prefer to avoid conflicts and those difficult conversations that are required when directly reporting employees do not complete their responsibilities. To build trust and encourage others to become leaders themselves, it is important to hold others to the highest standards they can reasonably be expected to attain.

Photograph by Randy Abbey

Abbey Family Photo Collection

*Photograph Courtesy of
Death To Stock Photographs*

16
Leaders Should Harvest What They Sow

September is one of those months associated with the harvest. Of course, in Arizona some harvests occur all year round. I grow tomatoes and herbs in the Spring before the heat of the summer, lettuce during the late Autumn, and citrus fruit during the Winter. Thinking about this and letting my thoughts wander to developing leaders, I was struck by the thought that leaders develop others by not only planting seeds of training and development, but also by harvesting the results of those training and development efforts.

When supervisors want to develop a trait or skill in someone, they frequently send that person to some type of training and development experience. It may be a conference, a college course, a workshop, seminar, or webinar. Then, they could simply say: "My job is done. I sent them to training, now it is up to them to do something with what they learned."

Alternatively, a leader will find ways to harvest the learning and development. How do they do this? By holding the trainee accountable for applying what they learned and by asking the trainee to teach others what they learned, the leader will reap the desired results.

It has long been a tenet of adult learning and training professionals that trainees retain more information and knowledge if they apply the learning or develop well enough to teach it to others. With this in mind I suggest that next time you send a staff member to a learning or training event, it should be required that the trainee return from the training and share their knowledge with others who were not able to attend the workshop, class, webinar, or conference.

Ask that trainee to teach you the information they learned as well, so you know what they can do to apply the knowledge on the job. Then, help hold them accountable for incorporating what they have learned. In this way, you will be not only planting the seed of training for your staff members, but also harvesting the learning and knowledge for your team.

Abbey Family Photo Collection

Abbey Family Photo Collection

17
Thanksgiving And Leadership

No, this is not my annual Thanksgiving blog. In fact, I haven't ever written a Thanksgiving blog before. One thing that has surfaced numerous times for me over the last few months goes back to research on the difference between management and leadership. One of the very simple definitions for this difference is that tasks or projects should be managed, while relationships or people require leadership. Another thing that strikes me about this difference is that task or process management can be honed to a skill-level that is remarkable in its ability to be replicated. Once a task is developed that truly works well, just follow the step-by-step guidance and the thing will practically manage itself. That is why detailed policies and procedures can be a good substitute for managers.

A bureaucratic organization with sound policies and specific procedures can eliminate middle managers by automating control systems to ensure policies and procedures work 90% of the time. The remaining 10% of the problems usually come down to human errors or failure to follow the process.

Leadership is different. It is all about encouraging, motivating, developing, and guiding people. Leadership is about building the relationships and the capabilities of people to go beyond the policies and procedures when necessary to truly innovate and take a product or service, company, or industry to a new level. Yes, that means sometimes failing, sometimes flailing, sometimes sailing, and sometimes soaring to new heights.

Thanksgiving, also is about relationships. It is about bringing people together, sometimes following generations-old traditions, and sometimes adapting to add something new and creative to the mix. Both management and leadership are important in business. Knowing when to step outside the boundaries of management in order to lead is the key to whether or not change will lead to failing or flailing.

18
Things Top Companies Do To Develop Leaders

I recently read HR Magazine's article about characteristics of companies who develop top leaders in the January/February 2015 issue. This article by Dori Meinert shares five characteristics that came from a survey of 180 companies conducted by Aon Hewitt in 2014. Below are my thoughts on the points made in the article.

<u>Assessment</u>. Leaders are assessed for development potential early in their career by companies who develop top leaders. Multiple leadership, personality, and behavior type assessments are available. For the most part any of these can be valuable if they are put to use for guiding and developing each individual based on his or her strengths and needed growth areas. In my workshops for supervisors and managers, as well as with my private coaching clients, we often use DISC, Myers-Briggs, Emotional Intelligence, or Strengths Finders assessments, depending on the client and their needs.

Self-Awareness. Leaders are encouraged to understand their unique strengths and weaknesses, not simply based on their own perception, but also based on how others perceive their actions. This is why 360 assessments that include self, subordinate, supervisor, client, and peer reviews can be exceptionally helpful. The key to using 360 evaluations is that they are used for growth and development of the leader, not for formal performance evaluation purposes. These 360 evaluations have the greatest potential when used for those in middle management positions or for individual coaching clients who may be struggling to move forward in an organization and desire insight into how they are coming across to others.

Empowerment. Leaders are empowered to be creative, innovative, and thoughtful problem solvers. Top companies never stifle the ideas and creativity of their employees who want to try something new, improve processes and programs, or grow and develop in new and innovative ways. Leading companies do not punish failure, but rather encourage informed, smart risk-taking. If a new idea or project doesn't turn out as the empowered leader hoped, the leader is encouraged to learn from the failure and to try something innovative again after applying the learning and problem solving that came from past mistakes.

Engagement. Companies that have top leadership development programs focus a great deal of time and energy on engaging their employees regardless of level, assessing engagement through employee surveys, and then taking action to remedy areas that are not conducive to engagement.

Strategic Performance Alignment. The top companies have clear strategic plans that focus on long-term sustainability of the company. Furthermore, they communicate openly and transparently to their employees at all levels about the company mission, vision, and goals; and they help each department, team, and individual connect their work goals to the company strategy. Rather than letting budget, status quo, or pet projects drive what gets accomplished on a day-to-day basis, these companies assess each work function and activity to ensure it is helping the company achieve the long term sustainable goals of the organization. They set measurable company performance goals, which are shared with their employees, so each person can do his or her part in helping the organization to achieve its vision.

*Photograph Courtesy of
Death To Stock Photographs*

19
Five Steps To Creating A Leadership Development Program

When I meet with a client seeking to create a leadership development program for the supervisors and middle managers of their organization, frequently they don't know how to get started. They realize leadership development needs to happen, and that their supervisors and managers were promoted largely because they were great at non-management activities, yet the task of transforming these managers into leaders seems too big to even know where to begin. The following steps provide a framework for how to proceed.

1. Determine what leaders in your organization need to do well in order to achieve your mission and advance toward the vision. These key leadership competencies will be the pillars of your development program.

2. Analyze the level of your current managers and supervisors in their practice of the key leadership competencies identified in step one.

What are your managers doing well, what are they struggling with, and what is not even on the radar screen for most of them? This analysis will tell you what gaps need to be filled to build a bridge from where your managers are now to where they need to be in order to lead your organization into the future.

3. Design the leadership development program to build skills around the key leadership competency pillars, using the information from your gap analysis to determine what level of learning your managers need. You may find some managers need to start at the very basics (even if they have been supervising for many years), while others may have some leadership acumen and simply need to hone or put into practice concepts they already understand.

4. Implement the program by developing and delivering courses, activities, experiences, coaching, mentoring, and any other methods necessary

based on the first three steps. Always use the key leadership competencies as the guide for which courses and development experiences to provide. Take care not to throw in any number of popular or feel-good topics that consultants may suggest simply because they are popular. Only those courses or learning experiences that align with the leadership pillars your organization needs should be included in the program.

5. Don't set and forget. Supervisors and managers will move through the program, learn fundamentals, begin putting these into practice, and move toward becoming better and better leaders. However, great leaders are always learning - they know that the world continues to change at a faster and faster pace, and that development may change shape, but never ends. Your program will need to be assessed along the way to determine if it is having the desired results, and whether or not additional competencies will be needed in the future. Monitoring, measuring, and

evaluating the performance of your leadership development program is often neglected; however, this is the key to success.

Abbey Family Photo Collection

20
Four Elements To Include In Your Leadership Development Program Design

Once you have determined the key leadership competencies required for a supervisor or manager to be successful in her leadership role within your organization, it is time to set about creating a unique program. You will need to assess where current gaps in skills exist, and prioritize training and development areas for your program's focus, but there are four elements to consider including in your program design.

1. <u>Foundational Learning</u>. This is the element that provides all participants regardless of their level in the company with a set of organizational principles, shared values, and a common language aimed at providing program structure. Foundational elements of learning may include ensuring participants understand the purpose for the leadership development program, the goals of

the program, how the program fits into the strategy and vision of where the organization is headed, and lays the ground work for future elements of the program.

2. <u>Level Adjusted Options</u>. This part of the program provides participants who have different levels of prior experience, skill, knowledge, and competence with level-appropriate learning, growth and development opportunities. For example, a high potential individual contributor with great industry acumen and technical skills who has never held a leadership or management role will have different training needs compared to a mid-level manager with many years of experience leading people, yet who is new to a particular industry. Both of these types of participant will also have very different development needs compared to an executive who is preparing to step into a C-Suite role. Providing two or three development tracks based on the levels of the participants is a great way to add

value to each group without dumbing down content or losing some participants who are new to leadership.

3. <u>Personal Development Plans</u>. Just as leadership development programs must adapt to groups at various levels, each individual has unique experiences, challenges, limitations, and growth and development needs. To help each participant maintain motivated and meaningful forward progress, it is a good idea to include a variety of opportunities for individuals to create their own personal development plans. Personal development plans might include a diverse group of options, such as attending specific courses, leading a team or a project outside the current scope of responsibility, working with a mentor, rotating into a new or different role, and other activities designed for each individual.

4. <u>Coaching</u>. Reflecting and reinforcing development through coaching is a great way to help the participant

transfer what they have learned to on-the-job situations. Often when a person attends a training course or motivational seminar, he or she commits to making intentional changes to achieve highest potential. However, making such changes can be difficult to sustain without the chance to reflect on the learning and growth lessons and to partner with a leadership and life coach who can reinforce the learning, be an accountability partner, and lend a fresh set of ideas to expand the rich possibilities for the individual. Without reflection and coaching a person can be successful, yet this is more difficult compared to those who have a coach or mentoring partner to help keep up the momentum.

Photograph by Michael Sultzbach

Photograph by Michael Sultzbach

Acknowledgements

There are so many people I need to thank, and I am sure I will mess this up and forget just about everyone who has helped me during this last year. So, if I miss thanking you publicly here please consider it first time author jitters, and know I will do better on my second publication.

Thank you to my amazing husband, Randy, who has been so supportive of my taking this leap. I must also thank him for his very kind and gentle help editing and proofreading. It didn't hurt a bit.

Thank you to my children who are reverse mentors and role models for me. I am in awe of them. If I believed in miracles, they would be named Alyssa and Alex.

Thank you Mike Sultzbach for taking such beautiful photos at our business launch party in January of 2015. It was fun to reminisce and use some of those pictures in this book.

Thank you to Connie Vonsleichter, my sister, who is also a number one reader and commenter on my blog.

Thank you to my clients, colleagues, and friends for believing in the dream, and for helping me to fill the world with leaders.

TWEETABLES

We would love you to share these tweetable quotes through your Twitter account, Facebook page, on your own blog, or anywhere else you would like. Plus, to help us touch the lives of more and more emerging leaders it would be awesome if you would include our website when you post or share: www.leaderdiscovery.com

"Once you know who you are as a leader, it takes a tremendous amount of work and even courage to trust yourself to lead based on who you are rather than who others expect you to be."

--Sandra Langford Abbey

"Leaders should use their strategic planning skills to implement personal resolutions in the same way business or organizational goals are achieved."

--Sandra Langford Abbey

"Choosing business relationships with care and cultivating them into supportive groups that also hold you accountable will impact your personal and professional life in profound ways."

--Sandra Langford Abbey

"Sometimes being a leader means plunging into new territory or making decisions without all the facts known."

--Sandra Langford Abbey

"Companies with little bench-strength can take advantage of succession planning when it is focused not only on top executives, but also includes developing leadership competencies at all levels of the organization."

--Sandra Langford Abbey

"Be watchful for emerging leadership traits from your employees or protégés. Catch them being innovative, trying something new, weighing alternatives before making a decision, collaborating ... taking responsible risks."

--Sandra Langford Abbey

"Because a leader by definition is someone whom others choose to follow, if a person is manipulated into furthering a goal and has not willingly chosen to follow someone, then no leadership has occurred."

--Sandra Langford Abbey

"The influx of the generation known as millennials may finally be what is needed to shift organizations toward flexibility."

--Sandra Langford Abbey

"Top companies never stifle the ideas and creativity of their employees who want to try something new, improve processes and programs, or grow and develop in new and innovative ways."

--Sandra Langford Abbey

"Monitoring, measuring, and evaluating the performance of your leadership development program is often neglected; however, this is the key to success."

--Sandra Langford Abbey

'Reflecting upon and reinforcing development through professional coaching is a great way to help the participant transfer what they have learned to on-the-job situations."

--Sandra Langford Abbey

Photograph by Michael Sultzbach

www.ingramcontent.com/pod-product-compliance
Lightning Source LLC
Chambersburg PA
CBHW041102180526
45172CB00001B/77